Discipleship Manual

SECRETS OF A
FRUITFUL
HEART

BOB SORGE

Oasis House
Kansas City, Missouri

INSTRUCTIONS FOR SMALL GROUP LEADERS

The parable of the sower is Jesus' model for discipleship. This parable helps us identify the issues that hinder our fruitfulness. The purpose of this Manual, when used in a small discipleship group, is to help us identify those hindrances. Once we identify the things that are hindering our fruitfulness, we can engage the process of overcoming them by His grace. As you participate in this study, you'll help others in the group become more fruitful disciples of Jesus.

Guidelines for Leaders

1. Everyone in the group should get a copy of both the Book and Manual. The Book can be used in either paperback or digital format, but everyone should get the Manual in *paperback* format for completing written answers. See FruitfulHeart.net for quantity discounts.

2. At each meeting, assign the next chapter in both the Book and Manual. Everyone should read the chapter in the Book, and then answer the Self-Reflection Questions in the Manual before the next meeting.

3. Everyone should bring both books to each meeting.

4. General format of each meeting:
   - Open with prayer.
   - Discuss your choice of questions in the Small Group Discussion section.
   - Close with prayer.
   - Assign the next chapter in the Book and Manual.
   - Mention the time and location of the next meeting.

5. During the discussion time, there's no pressure to get through all the questions. When fitting, you can take two meetings to cover one chapter—if the discussions are vibrant and meaningful.

6. Generally, you won't discuss the questions in the Self-Reflection section. Those answers are mostly personal between each person and Jesus. But exceptions can be made if the group wants to discuss one.

7. Work through all 26 chapters, as well as the Appendix, 27 chapters in all.

8. If the study is productive, please go to FruitfulHeart.net and submit a testimonial about what God did in your group. We'll post your testimonial to that page. You'll help other leaders understand how this study could benefit their small group.

9. After you've finished, study this parable all over again with another group of disciples. Work with Jesus and make disciples His way!

Guidelines for Closing Prayers

1. Close each group meeting with prayer. The group can:
   - Talk to the Lord about the content of that week's chapter, and how we're wanting to respond in obedience to the Lord.
   - Provide an opportunity for confession of sin.
   - Pray for specific needs in the group.

2. To help the disciples in your group grow, you'll want to provide opportunity each time for confession of sin, and then pray for one another, as James 5:16 says, "Confess your trespasses to one another, and pray for one another, that you may be healed." Confession and prayer for one another are foundational elements in making disciples of Christ. However, confession of sin is always voluntary, never obligatory.

3. A beautiful question to ask each person is, "Are there any areas of sin or struggle in your life that you want to confess, according to James 5:16, so we can pray for you?" You want to build a safe, non-judgmental culture in your group that promotes honest confession.

4. Here's one way to lead this kind of prayer around the circle of your group:

   1) The first person confesses any areas of compromise or struggle they want prayer for.

   2) The second person prays for the healing and blessing of the first person.

   3) The second person then confesses any areas of compromise or struggle they want prayer for.

   4) The third person prays for the healing and blessing of the second person.

   5) The third person then confesses any compromise for which they want prayer, and the fourth person blesses them with a prayer.

   6) Continue around the circle until all have opportunity for confession and until all have received prayer ministry from the group.

Chapter 1
Greatest Parable of All Time

SELF-REFLECTION QUESTIONS

A. In each SELF-REFLECTION section, write your own personal responses as you read through the book, *Secrets of a Fruitful Heart*. Your notes will be personal between you and the Lord.

B. As you launch this study on the parable of the sower, tell the Lord where you're at. What do you want Him to do in your heart during this study? Are there any areas of struggle in your walk with Christ that you want to make note of? Finish this sentence: "Dear Lord Jesus, as I come to this study, I'm asking You to

_____

_____

_____

C. Matthew 3:7-12 is quoted in Chapter One. Read the passage again and look specifically at all the metaphors in that passage: Vipers, fruits, stones, ax, root, trees, fire, winnowing fan, threshing floor, wheat, barn, chaff. Which of those metaphors strikes you most right now? Why?

_____

_____

_____

D. Jesus used several visuals in our parable—a field, a sower, a wayside, stones, and weeds. Do those visuals help you see and remember the parable better? Can you think of another teaching or story in the Bible that has spoken real strongly to you because of the visuals or metaphors in it?

_____

_____

_____

FOUR SOILS	HINDRANCE	MAIN ISSUE	CROP	TOOL
Trampled Heart	Birds	Unbelief	Stolen	Hoe
Shallow Heart	Stones	Tolerated Sin	Scorched	Shovel
Neglected Heart	Weeds	Distractions	Choked	Sickle
Fruitful Heart	All three	30/60/100-Fold	Productive	All three

E. Throughout this study, as we return repeatedly to the above chart, your understanding of the parable's message will grow. You'll realize that the parable's main message is found in the chart's third column. If there's something in the chart you don't understand yet, write your question. And if there's something enlightening in the chart, write what you're seeing.

_____
_____
_____

F. The word *parable* means *to throw alongside*. Thus, objects from everyday life are placed alongside spiritual truths so that our understanding of truth is enhanced. Look at Jesus' three parables in Matthew 13:24-33, and then choose one to examine more closely. List the objects in the parable, and what those objects represent. What is the parable's message? How does it apply to your life?

OBJECT	SPIRITUAL REPRESENTATION

G. The author calls this Jesus' *sledgehammer parable* because not all truth carries equal weight. For example, Jesus said that justice, mercy, and faith are weightier truths in Scripture than truths about tithes (Matt 23:23). Take some time to ponder Matthew 23:23, and write why you think Jesus called justice, mercy, and faith *weightier*. Why might you call the sower parable *weightier*?

_____
_____
_____
_____

1

H. Matthew, Mark, and Luke each tell this parable in full. They use 580, 476, and 329 words respectively. Matthew placed it in the center of his book to show that this was Jesus central parable. All three emphasize that Jesus delivered this parable when a large multitude had gathered. In fact, Mark used *multitude* twice: "And again He began to teach by the sea. And a great multitude was gathered to Him, so that He got into a boat and sat in it on the sea; and the whole multitude was on the land facing the sea" (Mark 4:1). Why did Jesus wait to tell this parable until a multitude was present? Are there any differences between the three accounts of the parable that you want to observe here? Are there any differences between the three accounts of the parable that you want to observe here? See Matthew 13, Mark 4, and Luke 8.

_____

_____

_____

SMALL GROUP DISCUSSION

(choose from these questions)

A. Do you agree with the author that the parable of the sower is the greatest of all parables? Why or why not?

B. A believer is someone who believes that Jesus is the Son of God and that He was crucified for us and rose from the dead. But a disciple is more than just a believer. A disciple is someone who is eager to hear and obey every word of Jesus. Jesus didn't commission us to make *believers* of all nations but to make *disciples* of all nations (Matt 28:19). What does this distinction between believers and disciples mean to you?

C. Was there a statement in Chapter One you'd like to highlight to the group?

D. During our times of group discussion, sometimes we'll ask whether there's a certain seed from God's word that has been working in your heart recently. In other words, is there a certain Scripture or scriptural idea that has been especially meaningful for you—something that you'd like to share with the group? Maybe it's a verse that has strengthened your faith or inspired your love. It can come from any place in your Bible reading. If the verse encouraged you, it may also encourage someone else in the group. In keeping with that, let's ask that question now. Is there a certain seed (word of God) that has been especially working in your heart this past week?

E. Look over the bullet points at the bottom of Chapter One in the book. Which of those motivates you most to become more fruitful?

F. Close in prayer. For suggestions on how to lead this prayer time, review the "Guidelines for Closing Prayers" on page 3.

   1. Express to the Lord what you're asking Him to do in your heart as you launch into this study. Ask for greater fruitfulness.

2. James 5:16 says, "Confess your trespasses to one another, and pray for one another, that you may be healed." Are there any areas of sin or struggle in your life that you want to confess, according to James 5:16, so we can pray for you? Ask each person in the circle. See the guidelines on page 3 for one way this can be done.

3. Is there a specific prayer need in the group?

4. Assign the next chapter in the Book and Manual, and remind everyone about the time and location of the next meeting.

NOTES

Chapter 2
The Parable Presented
SELF-REFLECTION QUESTIONS

A. Jesus commanded us to both see and hear this parable. Write down what you want to say to Him about hearing and seeing as you prepare to take this study to the end.

_____
_____
_____
_____

B. Song of Solomon 2:15 says, "Catch us the foxes, the little foxes that spoil the vines, for our vines have tender grapes." Foxes are small animals that damage the roots of plants by digging for grubs and worms. Has the Lord ever shown you any little foxes that have undermined your fruitfulness? How did you catch those foxes?

_____
_____
_____
_____
_____

C. Soil scientists estimate that there are, on average, around 140 weed seeds per pound of surface soil in cropland. That equates to approximately 200 million weed seeds per acre. What spiritual significance might you draw from that statistic?

_____
_____
_____
_____
_____

D. Jesus talked about thirtyfold, sixtyfold, and hundredfold fruitfulness. Does the potential for hundredfold make you want to become more fruitful? Or do you despair of ever becoming a more fruitful Christian? If the enemy lies to you about your fruitfulness, write down the lies he uses against you. Read each lie aloud, and then declare—*These are all lies!*

___

___

___

___

E. In another parable, Jesus spoke of a farmer who fertilized a tree (see Luke 13:8). Fertilizer promotes fruitfulness by rebuilding the soil. Farmers know they've got to have robust soil to have robust crops. Reflect on this question: What might be some fertilizers in the kingdom of God that strengthen the soil of our hearts and enable us to be more fruitful? Write your ideas, and any supporting verses that might come to mind.

___

___

___

___

F. My friend Mark Burlinson, who has a degree in soil management, said to me, "Suffering is the organic matter [fertilizer] that feeds our fruitfulness." Write any responses you might have to his statement.

___

___

___

___

G. Even a plant that was only thirtyfold fruitful was commended by Jesus. How does that speak to you of the way He views us when we're fruitful only in limited ways?

___

___

SMALL GROUP DISCUSSION

(choose from these questions)

A. Have you ever seen a flock of birds go after seeds on the ground? Tell the group where it happened and how it demonstrated the keen appetite birds have for seeds.

B. Have you ever seen garden vegetation that was scorched by the sun because of insufficient moisture? What stood out to you about it?

C. Have you ever seen a garden or field that was overgrown with weeds because the owner had stopped fighting them? Why do you still remember it?

D. Have you ever known people who bore no spiritual fruit because they had a trampled heart, or a shallow heart, or a neglected heart? Don't mention any names, but tell the group what you learned from their example.

E. From point E in the Self-Reflection Questions above, what kingdom fertilizers did you note that you might want to share with the group? Could we say that discipleship groups such as the one we're in right now can fertilize our hearts?

F. Is there a certain seed (word of God) that has been working in your heart this past week?

G. Closing prayer.
   1. Are there any areas of sin or struggle in your life that you want to confess, according to James 5:16, so we can pray for you?
   2. Ask the Lord to bless this discipleship group in a special way that, as we commit to one another for the next few months, our hearts might be strengthened by one another during this study.

H. Assign the next chapter in the Book and Manual.

NOTES

Chapter 3
The Purpose of Parables

SELF-REFLECTION QUESTIONS

A. When Jesus explained His use of parables in Mark 4:10-12, He said they were meant to both illuminate and hide. That's paradoxical. What's a paradox? A paradox is two truths that appear, on the surface, to contradict. But when they're placed side by side and examined, they provide for some of the strongest and sweetest insights about the kingdom of God. Perhaps that's why so much about Jesus was paradoxical. How many paradoxes from Jesus' teaching ministry can you identify and note here? With each paradox, what insights into truth does the paradox offer?

_____
_____
_____
_____
_____
_____
_____

B. The parable raises a fantastic question: *What is it about this parable that unlocks understanding to all the parables?* How might you answer that question?

_____
_____
_____
_____
_____
_____

C. Parables are holy invitations to go on in-depth explorations of the metaphors and meanings within them. Jesus delivered at least six other parables with agricultural metaphors (Matt 13:24-30; Matt 13:31-32; Matt 21:33-44; Luke 12:16-21; Luke 13:6-9). Choose one of them, write the reference, and then answer these questions: What are the various metaphors in the parable? What does each one mean? In what way does the parable of the sower help you understand the meanings within this other parable?

_____

_____

_____

_____

D. Look again at Mark 4:12. How do parables separate those who truly love the Lamb of God from those who don't? In Matthew 22:11, there was a guest who gained admittance to the wedding but had no wedding garment. Does that verse perhaps describe someone who gained entrance on a technicality but didn't actually love Jesus?

_____

_____

_____

_____

E. Psalm 12:6 says, "The words of the LORD are pure words, like silver tried in a furnace of earth, purified seven times." Every word God speaks has to sustain seven blasts of refining fire before He releases it. If He has tested each word in this parable with that kind of scrutiny, do you think it can hold up under our scrutiny? How does this affect the way you view Scripture? How authoritative is the word of God?

_____

_____

_____

_____

3 SMALL GROUP DISCUSSION

(choose from these questions)

A. The author describes this parable as a Master Key that unlocks understanding to all the other parables. How does this parable affect the way you look at other parables?

B. During the days of creation, when He created all the vegetation for our planet, Jesus already had His parables in mind. When Jesus created seeds and weeds and crops, do you think He intentionally designed them to embody spiritual truths?

C. Both Jesus and Paul spoke of *mysteries*. What do you consider to be the greatest mystery of Scripture that has been made known to us?

D. Was there a statement in this chapter you'd like to highlight to the group?

E. Is there a certain seed (word of God) that has been working in your heart this past week?

F. Did you think this week about a paradox in Scripture that you want to share with the group?

G. Closing prayer.
   1. Are there any areas of sin or struggle in your life that you want to confess, according to James 5:16, so we can pray for you?
   2. Ask the Lord for greater understanding into parables and paradoxes and mysteries of the kingdom.
   3. Does anyone in the group desire prayer regarding a concern you're carrying?

H. Assign the next chapter in the Book and Manual.

NOTES

Chapter 4
The Parable Explained

FOUR SOILS	HINDRANCE	MAIN ISSUE	CROP	TOOL
Trampled Heart	Birds	Unbelief	Stolen	Hoe
Shallow Heart	Stones	Tolerated Sin	Scorched	Shovel
Neglected Heart	Weeds	Distractions	Choked	Sickle
Fruitful Heart	All three	30/60/100-Fold	Productive	All three

SELF-REFLECTION QUESTIONS

A. As you look at the first two columns in the chart above, write down why a trampled heart is vulnerable to birds. Explain why stones will cause a plant to be shallow. And explain why weeds speak of neglect.

_____
_____
_____
_____
_____
_____

B. Jesus portrayed Satan as a bird that wants to steal the seed of God's word from us. Using an online Bible search program or a similar tool, look up the word *thief* in the Bible and read the verses in which the word *thief* (or similar words) occurs. (Note: Online Bible search programs can usually be accessed by typing a question into your Google search bar.) How many verses can you find in Scripture that refer to Satan as a thief? Write one down, along with any observations about how he tries to steal from us.

_____
_____
_____
_____

C. Can you think of a time in your life when the word of God haunted and troubled you, and now you realize that was a good thing? This parable is helping you realize that the seed of the word penetrated your heart on that occasion and the demons didn't steal it. Want to note the story here?

_____

_____

_____

_____

D. Can you think of anyone in the Bible whose life illustrates the Shallow Heart because they harbored stones of compromise? It might be someone who had a joyful response to God's word but soon afterwards stumbled. If you can think of someone, write their name down, the Scripture reference, the stones they harbored, and what you glean from their example.

_____

_____

_____

_____

E. Proverbs 24:30-31 is quoted in this chapter, take another look at it. The owner of the overgrown field was described as *lazy* and *devoid of understanding*. He was lacking in diligence and wisdom. Look at verses in Proverbs where the words *lazy, diligent,* and *wisdom* occur. Chapters 10 to 13 of Proverbs are especially laden with these words. Write out four verses that have one of these words in it. Why did you choose those four? How do they guide us to become more fruitful? (Besides chapters 10-13, you may also want to take a look at these verses in Proverbs: 4:5-7; 8:11; 9:10; 14:8; 18:4; 20:4; 21:5, 20; 22:13; 23:23; 24:3; 26:16.)

_____

_____

_____

_____

_____

SMALL GROUP DISCUSSION

(choose from these questions)

A. Tell the group about a time when your heart was trampled hard by a certain incident. What did you do about it?

B. The author suggests that the stones in the parable represent *pockets of sinful compromise*. When you view the stones as pockets of sin, does that help you understand the parable better?

C. *We're torn between the fruitful and the unfruitful.* Let's talk about that statement. How have you been torn between the two?

D. Jesus said, "But seek first the kingdom of God and His righteousness, and all these things shall be added to you" (Matt 6:33). What does it mean to *seek first the kingdom of God and His righteousness*?

E. What's the primary way you receive the implanted seed of God's word? Is it in your secret place? In church? Online? Tell the group what your favorite seed source is.

F. Was there a statement in this chapter you'd like to highlight to the group?

G. Closing prayer.

   1. Are there any areas of sin or struggle in your life that you want to confess, according to James 5:16, so we can pray for you?

   2. Let's pray for each person's secret place. Is there anything about your secret place relationship with Jesus you want prayer for?

NOTES

Chapter 5
Four Ways We Hear

SELF-REFLECTION QUESTIONS

A. Read the first three chapters of Revelation, and note the reference every time the word *hear* (or hears, heard, hearing) is used. Write your impressions of this word's significance in Revelation 2-3.

_____

_____

_____

_____

_____

B. The author wrote about the trifecta of heart transformation: seclusion, word immersion, and fasting. Have you dabbled at all with this trifecta? If so, write about your experience. Do you intend to pursue this trifecta in a more intentional way?

_____

_____

_____

_____

C. Do you agree that *hear* is the most important word in our parable? In the Bible? How is that word significant to you personally?

_____

_____

_____

_____

D. *All of us bear fruit to God based on how we hear the word.* Note your thoughts on this truth. What connection do you see between hearing and fruitfulness?

___

___

___

___

E. To observe the significance of *hear* in this parable, read Matthew's account of the parable in Matthew 13:3-23, and underscore all seventeen occurrences of *hear* (in its various forms). How does Matthew's emphasis on hearing shape the way you view the parable?

___

___

___

___

SMALL GROUP DISCUSSION

(choose from these questions)

A. *Everything in the Christian walk comes down to hearing and obeying.* That's quite a bold statement. Let's talk about it in our group. What does it mean to you?

B. Talk about what the author called the trifecta of heart transformation (seclusion, word immersion, fasting.) What do you think about the idea of getting away on a fasting prayer retreat?

C. In one of his sermons, Paul said, "For those who dwell in Jerusalem, and their rulers, because they did not know Him, nor even the voices of the Prophets which are read every Sabbath, have fulfilled them in condemning Him" (Acts 13:27). The Jews heard the prophets every Sabbath but yet never actually heard them. It's tempting for church attenders today to respond to the preaching of the word in a similar way. What are some things you've learned to do, that help you to really *hear* the word of God every time it's preached?

D. Jesus said, "My sheep hear My voice, and I know them, and they follow Me" (John 10:27). A lot of believers struggle with feeling like they don't hear God's voice. Can you share with the group any secrets you've learned to hear God better?

E. Was there a statement in this chapter that you'd like to highlight to the group?

F. Stephen said to the Jews, "You stiff-necked and uncircumcised in heart and ears! You always resist the Holy Spirit; as your fathers did, so do you" (Acts 7:51). What does it mean for God to circumcise our ears?

G. Closing prayer.
   1. Are there any areas of sin or struggle in your life that you want to confess, according to James 5:16, so we can pray for you?
   2. Let's ask the Lord to give us ears to hear His voice. Based on Acts 7:51, would you want to ask the Lord to circumcise your ears?

NOTES

Chapter 6
What Is Spiritual Fruit?

SELF-REFLECTION QUESTIONS

A. Examine the author's suggested definition of fruit: *Spiritual fruit is any godly deposit or quality that makes it into the age to come.* Note your comments on that statement. Does John 15:16 support it? If you have a definition for spiritual fruit that you think is better or clearer, write it down here.

_____
_____
_____
_____

B. When you think about *instant fruit*, the idea is so absurd it makes you grin. Fruit always involves a long growing season. Write down your commitment to endure with Jesus for the long haul, so you can eventually bear more fruit. Can you write a verse here that encourages you to endure in faith long-term?

_____
_____
_____
_____

C. Consider this passage: "However, the spiritual is not first, but the natural, and afterward the spiritual. The first man was of the earth, made of dust; the second Man is the Lord from heaven. As was the man of dust, so also are those who are made of dust; and as is the heavenly Man, so also are those who are heavenly. And as we have borne the image of the man of dust, we shall also bear the image of the heavenly Man. Now this I say, brethren, that flesh and blood cannot inherit the kingdom of God; nor does corruption inherit incorruption" (1 Cor 15:46-50). How does that passage help you value the things that are eternal rather than temporary? What does it mean to be a *heavenly man* just like Christ is?

_____
_____
_____
_____

D. Write down another verse you can find that compares the temporary with the eternal.

_____
_____
_____
_____

E. The author wrote about his relationship to his chainsaw. Is there something in your life that would be something of an equivalent—a pursuit in which you must restrain yourself?

_____
_____
_____
_____

F. Jesus said, "Even so, every good tree bears good fruit, but a bad tree bears bad fruit" (Matt 7:17). In the comparison between good and bad fruit, take a look at Jeremiah 24. In his vision, Jeremiah saw certain people depicted as rotten fruit. When you look over the course of your life, are there things in your past that you would identify as bad, rotten fruit? And now, as you consider the grace of God in your life, are there ways that you're now bearing good fruit to God? Can you write about it? Has God changed your nature and made you into a good tree?

_____
_____
_____
_____
_____
_____

G. John the Baptist warned his listeners, "And even now the ax is laid to the root of the trees. Therefore every tree which does not bear good fruit is cut down and thrown into the fire" (Matt 3:10). Write what that verse means, and how it challenges you personally. Write to the Lord what you want to ask of Him because of that verse. Tell Him how you need His help to bear good fruit.

_____
_____
_____
_____

SMALL GROUP DISCUSSION

(choose from these questions)

A. Spiritual fruit is any godly deposit or quality that makes it into the age to come. Talk about this definition and what it means to you.

B. Paul wrote, "For bodily exercise profits a little, but godliness is profitable for all things, having promise of the life that now is and of that which is to come" (1 Tim 4:8). Let's talk about how we view bodily exercise. When it comes to physical fitness, are you someone who needs to be more disciplined and purposeful, or more restrained? Do you have a story similar to the author's chainsaw story that you might want to share?

C. Paul wrote, "If then you were raised with Christ, seek those things which are above, where Christ is, sitting at the right hand of God. Set your mind on things above, not on things on the earth. For you died, and your life is hidden with Christ in God. When Christ who is our life appears, then you also will appear with Him in glory" (Col 3:1-4). Can you share with the group a practical way in which you've learned how to set your mind on things above?

D. We want to be more fruitful! And yet, Paul was torn between two desires. On the one hand, he wanted to be fruitful among the churches; on the other hand, he wanted to depart and be with Christ, which is far better. He expressed it this way: "But if I live on in the flesh, this will mean fruit from my labor; yet what I shall choose I cannot tell. For I am hard-pressed between the two, having a desire to depart and be with Christ, which is far better" (Phil 1:22-23). Do you also find yourself torn between the desire to remain here and be fruitful, and the desire to depart and be with Christ?

E. Is there a certain seed (word of God) that has been working in your heart this past week?

F. Closing prayer.
   1. Are there any areas of sin or struggle in your life that you want to confess, according to James 5:16, so we can pray for you?
   2. Express to the Lord your desire for heavenly things to hold a larger place in your heart.

NOTES

Chapter 7
Examples of Fruit

SELF-REFLECTION QUESTIONS

A. In what ways do you believe prayer has made you more fruitful? Psalm 110:3 said about Jesus, "In the beauties of holiness, from the womb of the morning, You have the dew of Your youth." In what way is your secret place the womb of your morning?

_____

_____

_____

_____

B. Every way in which we become more like Jesus is eternal fruit because we'll embody that quality of Christ *forever*. Look again at the fruit of the Spirit: "But the fruit of the Spirit is love, joy, peace, longsuffering, kindness, goodness, faithfulness, gentleness, self-control" (Gal 5:22-23). Write a short phrase of what each one means. Which of these nine are you especially asking the Lord to grow in your life right now? Why?

_____

_____

_____

_____

_____

_____

C. In what way do you feel you've been most effective in edifying other believers in the body of Christ? In what way do you want to become more skillful in edifying the body of Christ? Jesus said, "Abide in Me, and I in you. As the branch cannot bear fruit of itself, unless it abides in the vine, neither can you, unless you abide in Me" (John 15:4). Can you write of a way you've become more fruitful by learning to abide in Christ?

_____

_____

D. Look at number four on our list, *winning souls*. I once heard someone say that 70 percent of people born in the USA will never be invited to a church meeting in their lifetime. A statistic like that would suggest that many Christians in the USA are not active in the evangelistic pursuit of winning souls. How about you? How actively would you say that you pursue the winning of souls? Jesus said, "And he who reaps receives wages, and gathers fruit for eternal life, that both he who sows and he who reaps may rejoice together" (John 4:36). How do those words of Christ apply to the winning of souls? In what way is the Lord perhaps challenging you to be more fruitful in winning souls?

_____

_____

_____

_____

E. Jesus called money "unrighteous" (Luke 16:9, 11). Take a look at Luke 16:1-15. Do you think money is morally neutral, or do you agree with the author that there's something inherently evil about it? Does our answer to this question impact the way we relate to money?

_____

_____

_____

_____

F. Based on Ecclesiastes 7:12 and 10:19, it seems that unrighteous money has some positive aspects. What are they? Can you find any other verses in the Bible that place money in a positive light? How might you balance those with verses that warn against money's negative potential?

_____

_____

_____

_____

G. In 2 Corinthians 9:10, Paul described money as seed that, when sown properly, produces the fruits of righteousness. What are some ways that unrighteous mammon can produce fruits of righteousness?

_____

_____

_____

_____

SMALL GROUP DISCUSSION

(choose from these questions)

A. Let's talk about the five kinds of fruit listed in this chapter.
   - Friendship with Jesus in prayer
   - Christ-like character
   - Edifying the body of Christ
   - Winning souls
   - Exercising wise financial stewardship.

   In which of these five areas is the Lord challenging you most, right now, to grow in fruitfulness?

B. The question of whether money is morally neutral or morally charged is debated widely. What's your take on it? Can you tell of a time when the Lord taught you how to be more fruitful in your generosity?

C. Talk about your prayer life. How strong is it right now?

D. Was there a statement in this chapter you'd like to highlight to the group?

E. Is there a certain seed (word of God) that has been working in your heart this past week?

F. Closing prayer.
   1. Are there any areas of sin or struggle in your life that you want to confess, according to James 5:16, so we can pray for you?
   2. Let's ask the Lord to enable us to be more fruitful in the five ways that are presented in this chapter. Mention each in your prayers.
      - Friendship with Jesus in prayer
      - Christ-like character
      - Edifying the body of Christ
      - Winning souls
      - Exercising wise financial stewardship

NOTES

Chapter 8
More Examples of Fruit

SELF-REFLECTION QUESTIONS

A. Write down all ten examples of spiritual fruit mentioned in chapters six and seven. Can you think of any other examples that could be added to the list?

_____
_____
_____
_____

B. Look at number six, *Obedience to Jesus*. When we obey Jesus in faith and love, we bear fruit to God. Using an online search, can you find a Bible verse that expresses how pleased God is when we obey Him? Write it down here. Is there any command of Scripture you're struggling to obey right now? Put your struggle in writing.

_____
_____
_____
_____

C. Look at number seven, providing security for your household. Have you viewed earning money and paying the bills as a way to bear fruit to God? Do you view your employment as a way to be fruitful? While performing the duties of your occupation, do you find yourselves wanting to draw even closer to Jesus?

_____
_____
_____

D. In keeping with number eight (teaching our children in the Lord's way), what is something practical parents can do to teach their children in the word of God? Proverbs 22:6 says, "Train up a child in the way he should go, and when he is old he will not depart from it." Write down what that promise means to you.

_____

_____

_____

_____

_____

_____

E. Reflecting on number nine, when Christians suffer persecution, it's sometimes challenging to see how God is glorified through their suffering. But to God, you remind Him of Jesus. You're being reviled and persecuted just like Jesus was, and you're not reviling back. To Him, your love is beautiful, endearing, and fruitful. Talk to the Lord about Revelation 12:11, which says, "And they overcame him by the blood of the Lamb and by the word of their testimony, and they did not love their lives to the death." Tell Him that you don't love your life, even to death. Read Peter's story in Acts 5:26-41, and then let that be the backdrop for 1 Peter 4:13, "But rejoice to the extent that you partake of Christ's sufferings, that when His glory is revealed, you may also be glad with exceeding joy" (1 Pet 4:13). Peter was writing from personal experience! Make a note of your thoughts.

_____

_____

_____

F. Now we're on number ten, glorifying God. Take another look at the author's definition: *To glorify God is to cause people's esteem of Him to elevate.* If you like that definition, write down why. How do miracles and healings give glory to God? Do you desire for the Lord to be glorified through you in the ministry of divine healing? Can you write the story of a time when the Lord enabled you to glorify God in a special way?

_____

_____

_____

_____

SMALL GROUP DISCUSSION

(choose from these questions)

A. Five kinds of fruit are listed in this chapter.
   - Obedience to Jesus
   - Providing for our household
   - Teaching our children in truth
   - Enduring persecution
   - Glorifying God

   Which of these might you want to talk about?

B. Have you thought of any examples of spiritual fruit that could be added to the author's list of ten?

C. *A disciple is someone who is laboring to hear and obey everything Jesus commands.* Is that a good way to describe who a disciple is?

D. Romans 11:36 says, "For of Him and through Him and to Him are all things, to whom be glory forever. Amen." What does that verse mean to you personally?

E. *Nobody moves from thirtyfold to sixtyfold fruitfulness. Rather, we grow from thirtyfold to thirty-onefold.* In what way does that statement help you?

F. Have you ever been tempted to be a fruit inspector—that is, trying to figure out how fruitful another believer might be?

G. Let's talk about some of the ways believers are persecuted today. If you've ever been persecuted for your faith, tell the group about it.

H. Closing prayer.
   1. Are there any areas of sin or struggle in your life that you want to confess, according to James 5:16, so we can pray for you?
   2. *To glorify God is to cause people's esteem of Him to elevate.* Express to the Lord in what way you want to glorify Him more.
   3. Would someone want to offer a prayer to God based on this verse? "Being filled with the fruits of righteousness which are by Jesus Christ, to the glory and praise of God" (Phil 1:11).

NOTES

Chapter 9
The Birds

SELF-REFLECTION QUESTIONS

A. *Why are not all Christians hundredfold fruitful?* That's the overarching question of this study. Even before we explore that question together in upcoming chapters, write down how you might answer that question in this moment.

___

___

___

B. Every one of us is hassled by birds (demons) whenever we hear the word of God. Have you been aware of birds circling your heart? Or is this a new idea to you?

___

___

C. Take some time right now to visualize the wayside in the parable. Imagine that there's a hard patch of unbelief in a section of your heart, and then see the seed of God's word falling on that hard patch and bouncing. Then visualize the birds as they descend on that seed and have a meal. When you visualize the parable in this manner, what thoughts come to your mind?

___

___

___

D. *Unbelief is wordblock.* Write down your comments or insights on that statement. Can you think of a Scripture that carries that idea?

___

___

___

E. *You don't have a seed problem, you have a _____ problem* (fill in the blank). Write down why that statement is helpful.

___

F. What effect does soil compaction have on crop yield? If you do an internet search on that question, make a note of your answers.

G. Jeremiah 4:3 and Hosea 10:12 speak of breaking up our fallow ground. Look up those verses and the verses that surround them, and then write down what those verses mean to you.

H. Ask the Lord to show you any hard patches in your heart that are hindering your fruitfulness—that is, any way your heart responds in unbelief to God's word on a certain subject (e.g. healing, deliverance, provision, settling of fears, relationships, etc.). If He shows you an area of hardness, write it down here.

I. Here are some passages where Jesus and Paul spoke of a hard heart:

- "For the hearts of this people have grown dull. Their ears are hard of hearing, and their eyes they have closed, lest they should see with their eyes and hear with their ears, lest they should understand with their hearts and turn, so that I should heal them" (Matt 13:15).

- He said to them, "Moses, because of the hardness of your hearts, permitted you to divorce your wives, but from the beginning it was not so" (Matt 19:8).

- And when He had looked around at them with anger, being grieved by the hardness of their hearts, He said to the man, "Stretch out your hand." And he stretched it out, and his hand was restored as whole as the other (Mark 3:5).

- Later He appeared to the eleven as they sat at the table; and He rebuked their unbelief and hardness of heart, because they did not believe those who had seen Him after He had risen (Mark 16:14).
- But in accordance with your hardness and your impenitent heart you are treasuring up for yourself wrath in the day of wrath and revelation of the righteous judgment of God (Rom 2:5).

Choose one of those verses, and write your thoughts on that verse related to a hard heart.

_____
_____
_____
_____

SMALL GROUP DISCUSSION
(choose from these questions)

A. Why are not all Christians hundredfold fruitful? How might you answer that question?

B. Proverbs 20:4 says, "The lazy man will not plow because of winter; he will beg during harvest and have nothing." Are you ever tempted to be lazy, and not do the hard work of plowing the soil of your heart?

C. Unbelief is wordblock. Tell the group what that statement means to you.

D. Is there a statement in this chapter you want to highlight to the group?

E. In Luke's account of our parable, Jesus said, "A sower went out to sow his seed. And as he sowed, some fell by the wayside; and it was trampled down, and the birds of the air devoured it" (Luke 8:5). It wasn't just the wayside that was trampled, but according to Jesus it was also the seed that was trampled. In what way do you think the word of God itself can possibly be trampled in our hearts?

F. Is there a certain seed (word of God) that has been working in your heart this past week?

G. Closing prayer.

  1. Are there any areas of sin or struggle in your life that you want to confess, according to James 5:16, so we can pray for you?

  2. Is there an area of hardness in your heart that you want us to pray for?

NOTES

Chapter 10
Trampled by People Traffic

SELF-REFLECTION QUESTIONS

A. Look at the paragraph that starts with the sentence, "There are many ways believers can trample our hearts." What are some of the ways you've been trampled personally by the words, attitudes, or actions of other believers? Do you have a story to write about? Are you aware of a time when you also trampled another believer? Of the several kinds of trampling mentioned in that paragraph, is there one that you think happens most often?

_____
_____
_____
_____
_____
_____

B. Have you ever gotten in a political conversation with another believer and come away with a trampled heart? Feel free to note the incident. In retrospect, what did you learn from that incident? How can believers talk politics without trampling one another?

_____
_____
_____
_____
_____

C. If you're married, has there been any trampling in your marriage? Is there any way in which sin has been tolerated in your marriage? Write as much about it here as you might desire. What is the Lord saying to you about the best way forward? What can you and your spouse do to make your marriage a no-tolerance zone for sin?

_____
_____

D. Jesus said, "If your brother sins against you, rebuke him; and if he repents, forgive him" (Luke 17:3). Do you agree with the author that this verse can apply to Christian marriages? Write your thoughts.

E. Work, school, restaurants, stores, university, governmental institutions, recreation, where do you tend to get trampled most?

F. For the next week, practice the sprinkling of Hebrews 10:22 daily. Each morning, ask Jesus to sprinkle you with His blood, and then wash your body by reading and meditating in the word of God. Write down how meaningful and helpful this was for you. Did it soften your heart? Are you going to continue to practice receiving the sprinkling of blood?

10

SMALL GROUP DISCUSSION

(choose from these questions)

A. *People can trample your heart.* Talk about the things that come to mind when you read that statement.
   - Have you ever been trampled by slander?

B. *Christians can trample your heart.* What can we do, here in our small group, to guard from trampling each other with our words when we come together for this study?

C. Some of the people in this group may have lived through the upheaval of the international COVID-19 pandemic of 2020. What are some ways we can navigate similar times of upheaval within the body of Christ without trampling one another?

D. If you're married, how has the Lord helped you to avoid trampling your spouse with your words, actions, or attitudes? If you're single, how has the Lord helped you to avoid trampling your friends?

E. *Go after the sin in your marriage.* We could broaden it to say, *Go after the sin in your friendships.* Talk about what that statement means to you.

F. When your believing spouse has sinned against you, have you ever obeyed Luke 17:3 and rebuked them?

G. Is the sprinkling of blood, according to Hebrews 10:22, a meaningful practice for you personally?

H. Closing prayer.
   1. Are there any areas of sin or struggle in your life that you want to confess, according to James 5:16, so we can pray for you?
   2. Let's bless each marriage represented by the people in this group.

NOTES

Chapter 11
Trampled by Family and Friends

SELF-REFLECTION QUESTIONS

A. *Sometimes it's the people we love most who trample our hearts most.* In what ways has this happened to you, and in what ways do you think you've trampled those you love most?

___
___
___
___

B. Some people seem to get offended more quickly than others. Have you been tempted to be easily offended by friends and family? If so, how has the Lord helped you to overcome?

___
___
___
___

C. We're called to lose our lives, not save them (Matt 16:25). Self-preservation can cause us to insulate ourselves from others, which in turn hardens us to the implanted seed of God's word. Can you think of an incident where you were tempted with self-preservation? Can you think of someone in the Bible who was hindered spiritually because of self-preservation?

___
___
___
___

D. Offense distorts how we perceive the condition of our own heart, as well as the hearts of others. Jesus said, "And why do you look at the speck in your brother's eye, but do not consider the plank in your own eye? Or how can you say to your brother, 'Let me remove the speck from your eye'; and look, a plank is in your own eye? Hypocrite! First remove the plank from your own eye, and then you will see clearly to remove the speck from your brother's eye" (Matt 7:3-5). People often say today that we live in a *cancel culture*—that is, if we don't like what someone said or did, we'll readily reject and ostracize them. Have you been cancelled by anyone in our culture? Have you been tempted to cancel others? How have you learned to consider others better than yourself (Phil 2:3)?

E. *It's impossible for offended Christians to grow in fruitfulness.* Is there any way in which you've experienced that statement to be true?

F. In your formative years, did someone among your family or friends trample your heart, and do you still feel somewhat pained or bothered by the memories? What can you do to take a hoe to that hard part of your heart and make it soft again?

G. How has God redeemed the way you've been rejected by others, to make you the person you are today?

H. Review the ten statements about forgiveness at the end of this chapter, and write down the one that stands out most to you. Why is it meaningful to you?

_____
_____
_____
_____
_____
_____

SMALL GROUP DISCUSSION

(choose from these questions)

A. *Nothing hardens the heart faster than offense.* Do you have a story to share with the group about a time when offense tried to harden your heart?

B. Cancel culture hardens the heart. Jesus seemed to address cancel culture when He said, "And why do you look at the speck in your brother's eye, but do not consider the plank in your own eye? Or how can you say to your brother, 'Let me remove the speck from your eye'; and look, a plank is in your own eye? Hypocrite! First remove the plank from your own eye, and then you will see clearly to remove the speck from your brother's eye" (Matt 7:3-5). Living in a cancel culture, how can we keep our hearts soft?

C. Jesus said, "Whoever causes one of these little ones who believe in Me to sin, it would be better for him if a millstone were hung around his neck, and he were drowned in the depth of the sea. Woe to the world because of offenses! For offenses must come, but woe to that man by whom the offense comes!" (Matt 18:6-7). If a disciple, in their earlier years, caused a little one to sin, what can they do now to make it right before God?

D. The author uses the image of a hoe to picture the way we can soften areas of hardness in our hearts. Is there any area in your heart that you don't know right now how to soften, but you're resolved to keep swinging your hoe until it's softened?

E. How has God used the rejection of others to help shape your character?

F. Of the ten statements about forgiveness at the end of this chapter, which one would you like to talk about?

G. Is there a certain seed (word of God) that has been working in your heart this past week?

H. Closing prayer.

1. Are there any areas of sin or struggle in your life that you want to confess, according to James 5:16, so we can pray for you?

2. Pray for anyone in the group who may have experienced an offense or trauma in their childhood, and the memory of it still seems hard in their hearts. Confess the hardness as sin. Let's believe the Lord for healing.

NOTES

Chapter 12
Trampled by Beasts

SELF-REFLECTION QUESTIONS

A. What beasts of unbelief tend to harden your heart? Maybe it's a beast the author didn't even mention in this chapter. How does it help you to view trampling influences as *beasts*?

_____

_____

_____

_____

B. Much of the time we spend in media entertainment is fruitless in the kingdom. Think about the ways you consume media and streaming content. How have you learned to guard your heart from being trampled by the beasts of media? Is there a media beast you still need to overcome?

_____

_____

_____

_____

C. If you've ever battled depression, write about how the Lord helped you gain victory.

_____

_____

_____

_____

D. Have you found the maintaining of mountain-moving faith to be a delicate thing that is easily trampled by beasts of culture? What secrets have you learned to guard your faith? Is there one thing that tramples your faith perhaps more easily than anything else?

_____

_____

E. These two psalms talk about Jesus' footsteps:

- Your way was in the sea, Your path in the great waters, and Your footsteps were not known (Ps 77:19).
- With which Your enemies have reproached, O LORD, with which they have reproached the footsteps of Your anointed (Ps 89:51).

Can you write about a time when Jesus walked with you in a profoundly unique way? How did He bring you through? How long did it take you to understand why He walked with you that way?

_____

_____

_____

_____

F. Have you ever felt trampled by the way Jesus chose to walk with you? Have you ever been angry with God? Make a note about it here.

_____

_____

_____

_____

G. What is it about Judas Iscariot's story that stood out most to you while reading this chapter? He kissed Jesus because he thought he was doing Jesus a kindness. He had lost his ability to see his actions objectively. What had impaired his vision?

_____

_____

_____

_____

12

SMALL GROUP DISCUSSION

(choose from these questions)

A. The author applied the trampling beasts of the parable to today's media outlets. Let's talk about the way that media platforms can trample our hearts.

B. Besides media, what are some other beasts of our culture that can trample our hearts?

C. Do you think it's possible for our hearts to be trampled by the Sower? Do you have a story that illustrates this?

D. Can you think of a person in the Bible who got angry at God for the way He was walking with them?

E. Do you agree with the author that depression is a wayside problem?

F. This chapter closed with a section on Judas Iscariot. In your opinion, why do you think Judas betrayed Jesus?

G. Was there a statement in Chapter 11 that you'd like to highlight to the group?

H. Closing prayer.

1. Are there any areas of sin or struggle in your life that you want to confess, according to James 5:16, so we can pray for you?

2. Is there a certain cultural beast that you tend to allow to trample your heart more than you should, and you desire prayer? How can we pray for you?

NOTES

Chapter 13
How Can We Soften Our Hearts?

SELF-REFLECTION QUESTIONS

A. Repentance involves two things. What are they? What do they mean to you?

_____
_____
_____
_____

B. Why is repentance such hard work?

_____
_____
_____
_____

C. The author uses the image of a farmer's hoe to represent the way we break up our fallow ground. In what way does the metaphor of a hoe help you understand repentance and the breaking up of our hard hearts?

_____
_____
_____
_____

D. General William Booth, the founder of the Salvation Army, wrote in his memoirs about one of his leaders who was struggling at her post. She was frustrated that the work wasn't progressing, and she didn't know what to do. When she asked the General to assign her to a different post, General Booth replied with two words, "Try tears."[1] Do you remember a time when tears helped you move forward in God? If you've experienced a moment when tears helped you break up hard places in your heart, describe the experience.

_____
_____
_____
_____

---

1 "Try Tears," Make the Vision Plain (blog), https://makethevisionplain.com/try-tears

E. Do you practice the praying of Scripture? If not, can you find someone to coach you? And if you do, what practices help you most? The Hebrew word for *meditation* means to mumble over and over. Read the word, write the word, say the word, sing the word, and pray the word. Consider these Scriptures:

"This Book of the Law shall not depart from your mouth, but you shall meditate in it day and night, that you may observe to do according to all that is written in it. For then you will make your way prosperous, and then you will have good success" (Josh 1:8). "Let the word of Christ dwell in you richly in all wisdom, teaching and admonishing one another in psalms and hymns and spiritual songs, singing with grace in your hearts to the Lord" (Col 3:16).

With those verses in view, write down what you believe the Lord is saying to you about praying the Scriptures.

_____

_____

_____

_____

_____

F. What guardrails are you going to place around your heart so the beasts of our culture don't trample you?

_____

_____

_____

_____

_____

_____

13 SMALL GROUP DISCUSSION

(choose from these questions)

A. Do you think Christians eventually outgrow repentance, or is it something we practice all our days?

B. Let's talk about fasting, choosing from the following possible questions.

- Tell the group your experience with fasting. How much fasting have you practiced?
- You can talk about a Daniel fast, a juice fast, or a water-only fast. Which have you experienced?
- In what ways has fasting helped you?
- In what ways does fasting intimidate you?
- What secrets have you learned? How can fasting become easier?
- What does the Lord seem to be saying to you right now about fasting?
- Is there interest in our group to do a fast together?

C. Are tears easy or hard for you? Have you ever asked God for the gift of tears?

D. Was there a statement in this chapter you'd like to highlight to the group?

E. Closing prayer.

1. |Are there any areas of sin or struggle in your life that you want to confess, according to James 5:16, so we can pray for you?

2. We've looked at seven ways to soften our hearts:

    Repent.

    Weep.

    Forgive.

    Fast.

    Pray Scripture.

    Erect guardrails.

    Ask for rain.

    Which of these seven do you want to pray about? Is there a specific way we can stand with you in prayer?

NOTES

Chapter 14
The Stones

SELF-REFLECTION QUESTIONS

A. The stones in Jesus' parable represent pockets of sin that hinder our root development. Write about a time when the Lord showed you a stone of compromise in your heart. How did His grace help you dig up and remove that stone from your life? Have you gained victory over any other stones that has been so significant that you want to write about here?

_____
_____
_____
_____
_____

B. Have you ever seen a stone of sin in your heart but decided to live with it for a while? Is it still there? Write down whatever you want to say to the Lord about that stone.

_____
_____
_____
_____

C. Has a change of seasons ever surfaced a stone in your heart that you didn't know was there? What was the season change? What was the stone you saw? How did you overcome?

_____
_____
_____
_____
_____

D. Have you ever encountered a veritable *boulder* in your heart that loomed so large you didn't know how to get rid of it? Is it still there, or have you since gotten rid of it? Write about it.

___

E. Scripture speaks of talebearing (Lev 19:16), slander (Ps 101:5), gossip (1 Tim 5:13), and backbiting (Rom 1:30). Do you view these things as stones? What are some stones that are common to most Christians?

___

F. Do you believe increased persecution is coming to your nation? What do you see coming? How important will it be to have a stone-free heart in that day?

___

G. *Zero toleration for stones.* Express to the Lord, in writing, your holy resolve to keep your heart free of stones.

___

14   SMALL GROUP DISCUSSION

(choose from these questions)

A. If you're a gardener, and you've been surprised by a stone in your garden or yard, tell the group about your experience.

B. Why do changes of seasons cause stones in the ground to work their way toward the surface?

C. *The stormy change of seasons was a kindness!* Talk about what the statement means to you.

D. Have you ever found a stone in your yard that was bigger than you expected? Tell the story. What should we do when we find a stone in our heart that's bigger than we expected?

E. Secular counselors might show us ways to make peace with our stones and live with them. They may even want us to medicate our stones. Some medications are designed to lower our awareness of the stone's presence. Repentance, in contrast, is designed to unearth and remove the stones from the garden of our hearts. Have you ever found yourself in the tension between medicating your stones or removing them?

F. Look at Mark 4:16-17. "These likewise are the ones sown on stony ground who, when they hear the word, immediately receive it with gladness; and they have no root in themselves, and so endure only for a time. Afterward, when tribulation or persecution arises for the word's sake, immediately they stumble." Have you ever experienced a fiery trial that almost made you stumble?

G. *Greater heat, deeper reach.* How does that statement help you value the need for a deep root system in God?

H. Is there a certain seed (word of God) that has been working in your heart this past week?

I. Closing prayer.

   1. Are there any areas of sin or struggle in your life that you want to confess, according to James 5:16, so we can pray for you?

   2. *Zero toleration for stones.* Let's ask the Lord to release His grace to each one of us in this group, that we might hold firmly to this resolve.

   3. If there's a stone in your heart that you're still struggling with, this might be a good and safe time to tell the group about it. We're willing to pray with you!

NOTES

Chapter 15
Surprised by Fear

SELF-REFLECTION QUESTIONS

A. If you lived through the COVID-19 storm (2020-2022), what do you remember about the international hysteria? Did that stormy season surface any stones in your heart? If so, what were they, and how did you get rid of them?

_____
_____
_____
_____
_____

B. When you view anxiety as a stone, in what way does that help you fight against it? If you've ever been tempted to tolerate a stone of anxiety, write about it.

_____
_____
_____
_____
_____

C. "Be anxious for nothing" (Phil 4:6). What does that verse mean to you? Are there any other verses you like to use when you're resisting anxiety or fear? Write the verses here.

_____
_____
_____
_____
_____

D. *Anxiety engages in a battle for which there is no grace.* Write what that statement means.

_____

_____

_____

_____

E. Jesus waited until the day of His crucifixion (within 24 hours) to agonize in prayer over that trial. As you seek to follow His example, does this change anything about the way you engage with anxiety?

_____

_____

_____

_____

F. Ask yourself if you might have any fears or apprehensions related to the health history of your family. If you identify something, write down the medical condition and the person in your family who had it. Then write down what God's word says about that issue—you can write out a couple verses if you want. Is the Lord showing you something you can do to remove that stone?

_____

_____

_____

_____

_____

_____

G. When we find a stone in our hearts, what are some practical things we can do to dig up that stone? For example, one thing we can do is write down every verse in Scripture we can find that addresses that stone, and then meditate in those verses day and night. What else can we do to use our shovel on that stone?

_____

_____

_____

SMALL GROUP DISCUSSION

(choose from these questions)

A. Let's talk about COVID-19. You're welcome to share how the pandemic affected your life. What did you learn about fear in that season?

B. Let's talk about season change. Have you noticed that changes of season will surface things in your heart you didn't know were there?

C. Share with the group the Scriptures you like to use when you're resisting anxiety and fear (from C. above).

D. Jesus said, "Therefore do not worry about tomorrow, for tomorrow will worry about its own things. Sufficient for the day is its own trouble" (Matt 6:34). In what way does Jesus' example in Gethsemane inspire you?

E. If you fear that you might inherit a certain negative health condition from your ancestry, do you want to talk about it?

F. Was there a statement in this chapter you'd like to highlight to the group?

G. Closing prayer.
   1. Are there any areas of sin or struggle in your life that you want to confess, according to James 5:16, so we can pray for you?
   2. Is there a stone of fear in your heart you want to confess, that we might pray for you?

NOTES

Chapter 16
More Examples of Stones

SELF-REFLECTION QUESTIONS

A. Look at the sampling of stones the author mentioned in this chapter: Unforgiveness, anger, hatred, cynicism, addictions, dating an unbeliever, foolish talk, sexual sin, lying, rebellion, racism. Do you struggle with one of these stones? If so, which one?

_____
_____
_____

B. Do you struggle with a stone that hasn't been mentioned in this book? Write about your struggle, or about the way you successfully dug up that stone and removed it.

_____
_____
_____
_____

C. This chapter mentioned Ephesians 5:3-4, "But fornication and all uncleanness or covetousness, let it not even be named among you, as is fitting for saints; neither filthiness, nor foolish talking, nor coarse jesting, which are not fitting, but rather giving of thanks." It can be tempting for some, in particular those with a great sense of humor, to want to be the person in the conversation with a funny line or a great comeback. A quick tongue, however, can easily cross over into foolish or silly talk. Foolish talking will hinder our fruitfulness because it limits our stature in the body of Christ. Proverbs 10:19 says, "In the multitude of words sin is not lacking, but he who restrains his lips is wise." Based on these verses, what are your thoughts about foolish talking and silly banter? Is there another verse on this topic that you want to note?

_____
_____
_____
_____

D. *Porn is a stone.* Do you agree? Do you find it helpful to consider the viewing of porn as a stone? In what way? Make a note of your thoughts on this topic.

    _____
    _____
    _____
    _____

E. *When you see a stone, that means God is giving you grace to deal with it.* Do you think that statement is true? Can you identify a Scripture or Bible story that seems to support this principle? Have you actually experienced this?

    _____
    _____
    _____
    _____

F. What struck you most about the contrast between Judas Iscariot and Peter in this chapter? Why?

    _____
    _____
    _____
    _____

G. Look at Luke 12:1, "In the meantime, when an innumerable multitude of people had gathered together, so that they trampled one another, He began to say to His disciples first of all, 'Beware of the leaven of the Pharisees, which is hypocrisy.'"

    Judas Iscariot was present that day, so he heard Jesus' warning about hypocrisy. And yet, Judas persisted in his hypocrisy, acting as though his stones of compromise didn't exist. As a disciple, he was encouraging others to be obedient to God but was willfully tolerating disobedience in his own heart. What can we learn from Judas' hypocrisy? Have you ever been tempted to be hypocritical about your stones?

    _____
    _____
    _____
    _____

H. Have you ever gotten rid of a stone from your heart only to find another iteration of that same stone rising up sometime later? Write about it. Is it possible to have an issue in our heart that isn't just a solitary stone, but a series of pebbles we overcome as we see them?

_____

_____

_____

SMALL GROUP DISCUSSION

(choose from these questions)

A. The author mentioned cynicism in this chapter. What is it, how does it want to hurt us, and what can we do to get rid of it?

B. The author mentioned addictions in this chapter. Why is it that additions undermine fruitfulness? Are you struggling with an addiction you want to confess to the group?

C. The author mentioned sexual sin in this chapter. It's important for disciples of Jesus to confess sexual sin and remove it. We want every disciple in this group to overcome any sexual sin that is hamstringing their fruitfulness. If someone in our group struggles with a stone of sexual sin, how can they go about getting rid of that stone?

D. *The Christian life is not incessant introspection.* Let's talk about that statement. Have you ever been tempted to be too introspective in your walk with Christ?

E. *When God is giving you grace to overcome a stone of compromise in your heart, it's dangerous to ignore it.* Do you want to tell the group about a time when you were tempted to ignore a stone that was in the garden of your heart?

F. Satan had to ask permission to sift Peter, but Satan entered Judas uninvited. How does that difference speak to you?

G. The author suggested that demonic energy can attach to stones we tolerate in our lives. Do you have any understanding on this?

H. Was there a statement in this chapter that you'd like to highlight to the group?

I. Closing prayer.

1. Are there any areas of sin or struggle in your life that you want to confess, according to James 5:16, so we can pray for you?

2. To say it another way, do you desire prayer regarding any stone in the garden of your heart?

NOTES

Chapter 17
The Weeds

SELF-REFLECTION QUESTIONS

A. The seeds of weeds fly everywhere because of the wind. In terms of spiritual application, what do you suppose might be the winds that blow seeds of weeds onto our lives?

_____
_____
_____

B. Jesus said that weeds *choke*. Do have any experience with gardening or yard work? Have you seen weeds choke the life out of good vegetation around them?

_____
_____
_____

C. The author said that weeds always come back. Have you experienced this around your yard? Have you experienced this in your heart? Can you name an issue that you thought you had victory over, only to have it return repeatedly?

_____
_____
_____
_____

D. When stones are removed from a garden, they're gone; but when weeds are removed from a garden, they always return. Does that distinction help you understand the nature of the weeds that keep resurfacing in your heart? How does this help you control your weeds?

_____
_____
_____
_____

E. In this chapter, the author introduced the imagery of a *sickle*. When you visualize yourself swinging a sickle, how does that image help you in your fight with cares, riches, and pleasures?

F. In what ways can weeds actually serve a useful purpose?

G. *The weeds are cares and pleasures.* The difficult and the enjoyable. What are some difficult things in life that can easily overwhelm your time? What are some enjoyable things in life that easily distract you from being fruitful?

H. Weeds grow most vigorously during the season when the good plants are also growing most vigorously. Perhaps we could say we're tempted by the weeds of money and pleasure most when we're in our seasons of greatest increase. Have you experienced this? Are you tempted by money most in seasons of increase?

I. *The fruitless wants to choke the fruitful.* What comes to mind when you read that?

17 SMALL GROUP DISCUSSION

(choose from these questions)

A. Have you ever had to weed a garden? Tell the group what it was like.

B. Weeds are all plant and no fruit. Is it possible for a Christian to have lots of foliage but little fruit? Is it possible for a local church to have lots of branches but little fruit?

C. Let's talk about the way weeds always come back. As you walk with Christ, is there an area of struggle that seems to resurface over and over?

D. *Weeds are temporary things that choke eternal fruit.* Can you think of an example of something in life that is temporary and has the potential to choke eternal fruit in your life?

E. As you glance over the five observations about weeds in this chapter, is there something there that you want to talk about?
   - Every garden gets them.
   - Weeds dominate.
   - Weeds take a lot of work to suppress.
   - Weeds always come back.
   - Weeds are helpful in the right context.

F. *Weeds are temporary elements that make life in this passing world workable and enjoyable.* Do you like that summary statement?

G. Something about weeds: They can spread from one garden to another. Are there some weeds that we can pick up from other people? For example, Hebrews 12:15 says, "Looking carefully lest anyone fall short of the grace of God; lest any root of bitterness springing up cause trouble, and by this many become defiled." That verse describes a root of bitterness that seems to spread from garden to garden, from person to person, spreading defilement. Are there ways we should guard against roots and weeds spreading to us from others around us?

H. Was there a statement in this chapter you'd like to highlight to the group?

I. Closing prayer.
   1. Are there any areas of sin or struggle in your life that you want to confess, according to James 5:16, so we can pray for you?
   2. Would anyone like prayer for a weed in your heart that you've identified but has been difficult to treat?

NOTES

Chapter 18
Deceitfulness of Riches

SELF-REFLECTION QUESTIONS

A. Greek *cares* means *to divide the mind*. Can you identify some ways your heart gets divided because of the pressures, demands, and cares of life? What are two things that pull at your heart at the same time?

_____
_____
_____
_____

B. *The temporary can easily choke the eternal in our lives.* Write down some ways that temporary things try to squeeze out eternal pursuits in your life.

_____
_____
_____
_____
_____
_____

C. In what way does the image of a sickle help you visualize what you must do with your weeds?

_____
_____
_____

D. According to one survey, covetousness is the number-one temptation believers struggle with. Is it a temptation for you? Write down the way you might define covetousness. Covetousness is…

_____
_____
_____
_____

E. *Money lies to you.* What's the foremost lie that money tries to feed you?

F. Read 2 Kings 5. What can we learn from Gehazi's covetousness? Write down any lessons you glean from the story.

G. Read Acts 5. Ananias and Sapphira have this in common with Judas Iscariot: Their covetousness killed them. What else might their stories have in common? Is it safe to say that covetousness kills?

H. Paul wrote, "But know this, that in the last days perilous times will come: For men will be lovers of themselves, lovers of money" (2 Tim 3:1-2). The author confessed that he's sometimes tempted with the love of money. How about you? How does it tempt you? How do you cut back its tendrils?

I. Covetousness was the primary sin that overtook Lucifer's heart (see Ezek 28:16). His covetousness led to violence. We might say, then, that it was the first sin. Lucifer was given so much and yet wasn't satisfied. Find a Scripture about contentment, write it down here, and explain how it speaks to you. (Hint: Heb 13:5 is a good one.)

_____
_____
_____
_____
_____

J. Look at these two proverbs:

"The wicked covet the catch of evil men, but the root of the righteous yields fruit" (Prov 12:12). "An inheritance gained hastily at the beginning will not be blessed at the end" (Prov 20:21).

In 20:21, we're warned against hoping for a sudden financial windfall. Rather, in 12:12, we're encouraged to seek the kind of monetary reward that comes incrementally through daily, disciplined, rigorous cultivation. God wants our lives to be like a fruitful plant. Compare the two verses and note your observations.

_____
_____
_____

K. If you have time for an interesting study, look at all the mentions of money and riches in the Gospel of Luke. Luke highlighted this theme in Jesus' teachings more than the other Gospel writers. Write down the verses and your discoveries in the NOTES section.

SMALL GROUP DISCUSSION

(choose from these questions)

A. *Am I doing something right now that is temporary or eternal?* Do you ever ask yourself that question in the course of daily activities?

B. How do you keep the cares of life from overgrowing your heart?

C. Do you have a story about a time when you were able to do the will of God, even though you lacked finances?

D. *When it comes to money, never trust your heart.* Is that good advice?

E. *Money is a weed.* When you view money as a weed that needs to be kept on the periphery of our heart, is that helpful to you?

F. Jesus said, "But rather give alms of such things as you have; then indeed all things are clean to you" (Luke 11:41). In what way does that verse speak to you

G. Do you have a story related to generosity that you want to tell the group?

H. Someone once said that one of the first symptoms of backsliding is that people compromise on tithing, offerings, and almsgiving. Is that observation valid?

I. Closing prayer.

1. Are there any areas of sin or struggle in your life that you want to confess, according to James 5:16, so we can pray for you?

2. Let's pray together about our relationship to money. Does anyone in the group have any specific prayer requests related to this?

NOTES

Chapter 19
Desires for Other Things

SELF-REFLECTION QUESTIONS

A. The author said *the cares of this world* are all about making life *workable*, and *the desires for other things* are about making life *enjoyable*. Do you find that workable/enjoyable distinction helpful? In what way can the desire for an enjoyable life be a weed that chokes?

_____

_____

_____

_____

B. Free time sometimes opens to idleness. Do a brief study on what the Bible says about idleness. Include Ezekiel 16:49 in your study. Idleness is a weed. In what way do you personally need to guard against idleness?

_____

_____

_____

_____

C. When it comes to the weed of shopping for new stuff, how strongly does that weed tempt you? How has the Lord helped you with it? What are your thoughts about selling a possession and giving the proceeds to the poor?

_____

_____

_____

_____

D. Jesus said, "Remember Lot's wife" (Luke 17:32). What is it about her that you need to remember the most?

_____
_____
_____

E. *Lot was the righteous man in the Bible who lost his sense of journey.* Write out 2 Peter 2:7. How does this statement about Lot challenge your life personally?

_____
_____
_____
_____
_____

F. The author suggested that pride is a weed. How can we swing our sickle on that weed and fight for humility?

_____
_____
_____

G. As you think about comparisons, look at these two verses:

"But let each one examine his own work, and then he will have rejoicing in himself alone, and not in another" (Gal 6:4).

"Let nothing be done through selfish ambition or conceit, but in lowliness of mind let each esteem others better than himself" (Phil 2:3).

Write down how you see these verses speaking to the weed of comparison. In what way are you tempted to compare yourself?

_____
_____
_____
_____

H. The author defines weeds as areas of struggle that we gain victory over, but then they often return later and we must cut them back again. What sin might you struggle with that you would consider a weed?

_____

_____

_____

I. James wrote, "Where do wars and fights come from among you? Do they not come from your desires for pleasure that war in your members? You lust and do not have. You murder and covet and cannot obtain. You fight and war. Yet you do not have because you do not ask. You ask and do not receive, because you ask amiss, that you may spend it on your pleasures. Adulterers and adulteresses! Do you not know that friendship with the world is enmity with God? Whoever therefore wants to be a friend of the world makes himself an enemy of God" (James 4:1-4). Why would James say that the desires for pleasure would cause wars and fights among them?

_____

_____

_____

SMALL GROUP DISCUSSION

(choose from these questions)

A. The use of our electronic devices falls, in a way, under the category of *pleasures of life*. As you pursue greater fruitfulness, has that pursuit affected the way you use your devices? Got any secrets to share for overcoming?

B. When it comes to *desires for other things*, is there a certain desire that tries to choke your fruitfulness? Perhaps someone else in the group can tell how they found victory in that area.

C. *Lot was the righteous man in the Bible who lost his sense of journey.* Is there anything about Lot and his wife that you want to talk about?

D. Let's talk about comparison. *Comparison is a weed.* In what way has this weed tried to choke your heart?

E. Read 2 Peter 1:5-8 together.

"But also for this very reason, giving all diligence, add to your faith virtue, to virtue knowledge, to knowledge self-control, to self-control perseverance, to perseverance godliness, to godliness brotherly kindness, and to brotherly kindness love. For if these things are yours and abound, you will be neither barren nor unfruitful in the knowledge of our Lord Jesus Christ."

Peter indicated that adding these things to our lives will produce more fruit. Talk about Peter's list of faith, virtue, knowledge, self-control, perseverance, godliness, brotherly kindness, and love. How can we add more of these virtues to our lives?

F. Was there a statement in this chapter you'd like to highlight to the group?

G. Is there a certain seed (word of God) that has been working in your heart this past week?

H. Closing prayer.

1. Are there any areas of sin or struggle in your life that you want to confess, according to James 5:16, so we can pray for you?

2. Is anyone in the group wanting prayer regarding a struggle with a certain weed?

3. Is anyone wanting help from the Lord to overcome comparison, or envy, or the fear of man?

NOTES

Chapter 20
Three Stages of Fruitfulness

SELF-REFLECTION QUESTIONS

A. Are you finding, as you immerse yourself in the parable, that you're incentivized by Jesus to mature and become more fruitful? Write down how He's motivating you.

_____

_____

_____

B. A friend once said they saw the three stages of fruitfulness reflected in the three Jewish feasts of Passover, Pentecost, and Tabernacles. Do you have any comments about that to write here? Are there any other triads in Scripture that you think might correspond to thirty/sixty/hundred?

_____

_____

_____

_____

C. Paul seemed to nuance the word *mystery* a little bit differently from Jesus. For Paul, a mystery was a truth that was present but hidden in the Old Testament, and that did not come into clear view until Christ sent the Holy Spirit to help us understand. Look up the times Paul used *mystery* in his Epistles (such as Rom 16:25; 1 Cor 4:1; Eph 3:3-9, et al), and write down what you think he meant by that term.

_____

_____

_____

_____

D. Has the Lord ever shown you a mystery that is hidden in one of His parables? If so, make a note of it here.

_____

_____

_____

E. Although only in his thirties, Joseph spoke to his brothers of his spiritual fatherhood in this way: "So now it was not you who sent me here, but God; and He has made me a father to Pharaoh, and lord of all his house, and a ruler throughout all the land of Egypt" (Gen 45:8). Have you ever experienced a "Joseph-like prison" that accelerated your spiritual maturity? In what ways have you gained personal encouragement from Joseph's prison?

_____

_____

_____

_____

_____

_____

Three Stages of Fruitfulness

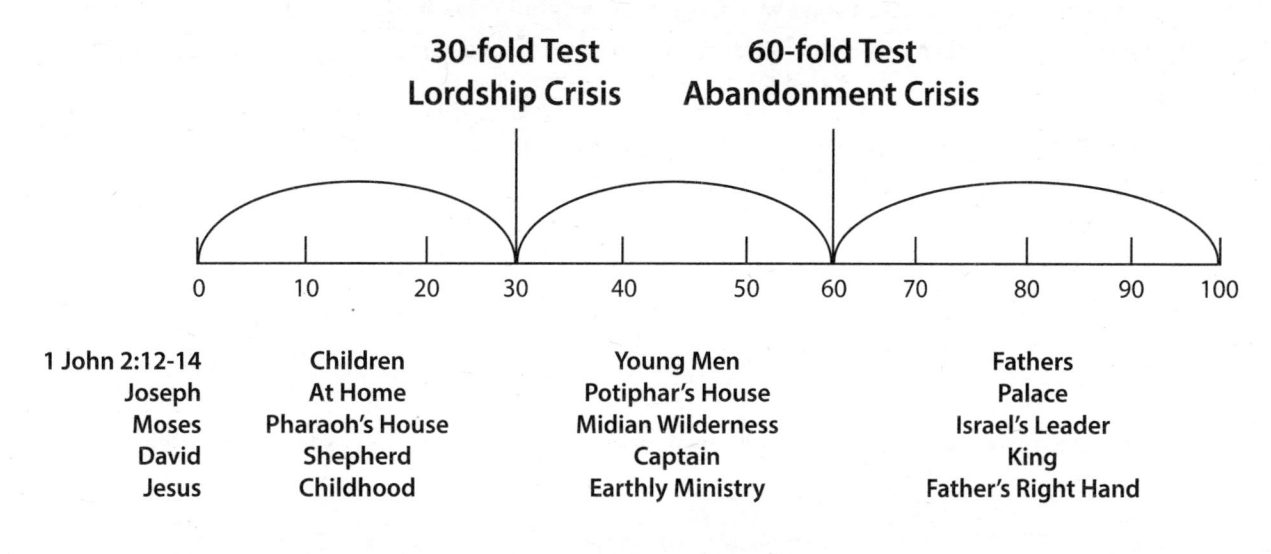

30-fold Test
Lordship Crisis

60-fold Test
Abandonment Crisis

1 John 2:12-14	Children	Young Men	Fathers
Joseph	At Home	Potiphar's House	Palace
Moses	Pharaoh's House	Midian Wilderness	Israel's Leader
David	Shepherd	Captain	King
Jesus	Childhood	Earthly Ministry	Father's Right Hand

F. As you examine the above chart, write down your observations, thoughts, or questions about it.

_____

_____

_____

SMALL GROUP DISCUSSION

(choose from these questions)

A. Let's talk about Chart 2. Is there anything you might want to say about this chart to the group?

B. *Nobody goes from thirtyfold to sixtyfold fruitfulness. We go from thirty to thirty-one.* Let's talk about incremental growth in fruitfulness. Was there a way in which you found that statement helpful?

C. *Kingdom mysteries are spiritual truths that are not readily evident at first observation, but can be mined and discovered through diligent digging.* When you want to dig deeper into biblical truths, what are some of the tools that help you? Share with the group the books, software, apps, or sites you find most helpful in study.

D. *Every parable of Jesus' was an invitation to explore.* Is there another parable of Jesus' that you've enjoyed exploring, or have a desire to explore?

E. Have you ever known someone who was comparatively young in chronological years but had already become a spiritual father or mother in the body of Christ? Did God accelerate their maturity?

F. From B. of the self-reflection questions above, do you want to talk about any triads you noted that may possibly correspond to thirty/sixty/hundred?

G. Is there a certain seed (word of God) that has been working in your heart this past week?

H. Closing prayer.
   1. Are there any areas of sin or struggle in your life that you want to confess, according to James 5:16, so we can pray for you?
   2. Does anyone have a need for which we can pray?

NOTES

Chapter 21
Little Children, Young Men, Fathers

SELF-REFLECTION QUESTIONS

Three Stages of Fruitfulness

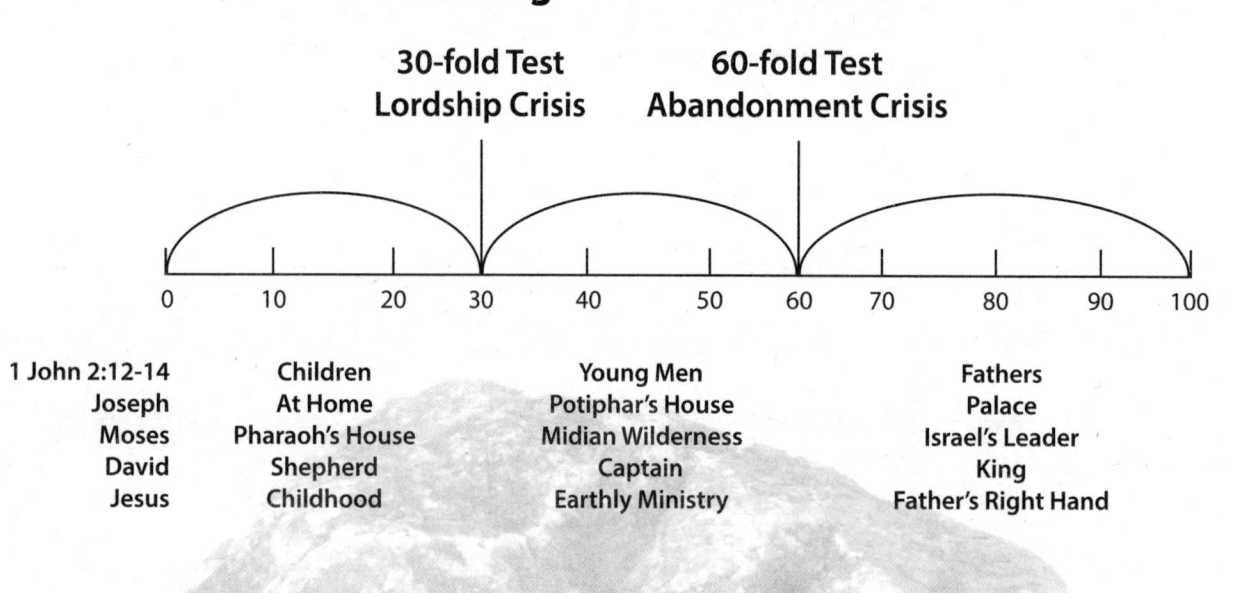

```
                30-fold Test           60-fold Test
               Lordship Crisis       Abandonment Crisis
                      |                     |
        _____   |   _____       |   _____
       /           \  |  /           \      |  /           \
    |---|---|---|---|---|---|---|---|---|---|
    0   10  20  30  40  50  60  70  80  90  100
```

1 John 2:12-14	Children	Young Men	Fathers
Joseph	At Home	Potiphar's House	Palace
Moses	Pharaoh's House	Midian Wilderness	Israel's Leader
David	Shepherd	Captain	King
Jesus	Childhood	Earthly Ministry	Father's Right Hand

A. *It's great to be a baby! It's just not great to stay a baby.* Can you think of an unfortunate medical condition that might possibly cause someone's natural maturing process to be hindered? Are there unhealthy spiritual conditions that can hinder our spiritual development?

_____
_____
_____

B. Paul wrote, "That I may know Him and the power of His resurrection, and the fellowship of His sufferings, being conformed to His death, if, by any means, I may attain to the resurrection from the dead" (Phil 3:10-11). Like Paul, we want to know God! Can you find any other verses in the Bible that express a similar desire to know God more? Write the verses here, and any comments you might have.

_____
_____
_____

C. *Fathers have experienced hard things, darkness, loneliness, resistance, despondency, grief, affliction, betrayal, and loss.* Have you watched someone go through these kinds of experiences and now you realize that God was preparing them for spiritual motherhood or fatherhood? Write any observations about how they walked the journey with God.

_____

_____

_____

_____

D. *Believers are saved en masse, disciples are made in small groups, and fathers are fashioned in solitude.* In what way might that statement align with your experience? Disciples are made, but fathers are fashioned. Can you think of a spiritual father or mother in the Bible who was fashioned by God in solitude?

_____

_____

_____

_____

E. How can we enter into fruitfulness that comes by the Spirit of the Lord instead of our own strength? Write down Zechariah 4:6 here. In what way has the Lord taught you not to lean on your own strength?

_____

_____

_____

_____

F. *The life stories of many devout saints divide naturally into three stages of maturity or fruitfulness.* Do you agree with this thesis? Is there anything about it that helps you? Can you think of someone in the Bible not mentioned by the author but whose life also divides into three stages?

_____

_____

_____

_____

SMALL GROUP DISCUSSION

(choose from these questions)

A. Do you know someone who fits perfectly into John's description of *young men*? That is, they're *strong, and the word of God abides in them, and they have overcome the wicked one.* Would it be appropriate to mention their name? Maybe they're even here in our small group?

B. What do you think John meant when he said that fathers are those who *have known Him who is from the beginning*?

C. In the final section, Examples of Three Stages, the author cited the examples of Joseph, Jesus, Abraham, David, Moses, Jacob, Job, Paul, Mordecai, Naomi, and Zacharias. Which example caught your interest most, and why? (There may be different answers within the group.)

D. Was there a statement in this chapter that you'd like to highlight to the group?

E. Is there a certain seed (word of God) that has been working in your heart this past week?

F. Closing prayer.

  1. Are there any areas of sin or struggle in your life that you want to confess, according to James 5:16, so we can pray for you?

  2. Let's close by praying for anyone in the group who might feel a little bit stuck in their current stage of fruitfulness, but who wants to keep moving forward with God. In what way do you feel stuck?

NOTES

Chapter 22
Two Crisis Points

SELF-REFLECTION QUESTIONS

A. Read Genesis 22:1-19. When you view Mt. Moriah as the place where Abraham passed the Abandonment Crisis, how does that shape the way you view the story? What would you identify as some of the elements that were operating in Abraham's Abandonment Crisis? (e.g., Abraham had to obey the Voice.)

_____
_____
_____
_____
_____
_____

B. This chapter mentions the sixtyfold crisis in the lives of Joseph, Jesus, Abraham, David, Moses, Jacob, Job, Mordecai, Naomi, and Zacharias. Are there any elements in their sixtyfold crisis that are common to several of the stories? Which crisis crossing grabs you most?

_____
_____
_____
_____
_____
_____

C. *The journey of saints in Scripture often involved two crisis points, with the second one opening to hundredfold fruitfulness.* Although we face many trials in life, have you understood that some believers face two especially big ones? How does this align with your own experience? Can you identify two big trials in your story, or is your journey not quite that tidy?

_____
_____
_____

D. At the thirtyfold crisis, we might expect God to call us to something miserable, and then we discover our obedience opens to some of the most satisfying territory we've ever inhabited. Have you ever experienced anything like this? Write about it.

E. *At the sixtyfold crisis, however, He actually takes it away.* That idea is based primarily on Job 1:21, "The LORD gave, and the LORD has taken away; blessed be the name of the LORD." Look again at our list of Joseph, Jesus, Abraham, David, Moses, Jacob, Job, Mordecai, Naomi, and Zacharias. Choose one of them, and write down what God took away from them at their sixtyfold crisis. Do you have a personal story to note as well, of a time when God took something away from you? Has He restored it yet?

22 SMALL GROUP DISCUSSION

(choose from these questions)

A. Do you have two crisis points in your life that seem to correspond to the two crisis points mentioned in this chapter? If so, you're welcome to tell the group your story.

B. Talk about the two crisis points in Joseph's life. In what way do you gain personal encouragement from Joseph's example?

C. When you view the cross as the thing that transitioned Jesus into hundredfold fruitfulness, does that affect how you view Jesus' invitation to you to take up your cross?

D. Like the previous chapter, this chapter also cites the stories of Joseph, Jesus, Abraham, David, Moses, Jacob, Job, Mordecai, Naomi, and Zacharias. Each of them faced a sixtyfold crisis. Which person's sixtyfold crisis might you want to talk about?

E. In this chapter the author mentioned self-determination. Have you had a time in your life when the Lord invited you to lay down your tendency toward self-determination and surrender instead to His sovereign leading in your life?

F. Was there a statement in this chapter that you'd like to highlight to the group?

G. Closing prayer.
   1. Are there any areas of sin or struggle in your life that you want to confess, according to James 5:16, so we can pray for you?
   2. Pray for anyone in the group who feels they're facing one of their two crisis points right now.

NOTES

Chapter 23
Emotional Elements of the Sixtyfold Crisis

SELF-REFLECTION QUESTIONS

A. This chapter said this about wilderness: *There's a painful disconnect between the promises you hold and the land you inhabit.* Is there any way in which you feel a disconnect right now between the promises you cherish and the attainments you're actually living in? Note any way in which you feel like you're in a wilderness right now.

_____

_____

_____

_____

B. *The anointing on your life is stronger than your current responsibilities.* In 1 Samuel 16:13, David was anointed to be king over Israel, and yet he spent years in wildernesses running for his life. Have you ever had a season where the anointing on your life was stronger than your responsibilities? Note any ways you might relate to that wilderness season in David's life.

_____

_____

_____

_____

C. Like Jacob, sometimes we're *left alone* so that God can do His intended work in our lives. Is there someone in the Bible who was left alone by God for a specific purpose, whose story you especially appreciate? How has God used loneliness or aloneness in your life? What's the greatest pearl you've gleaned through loneliness?

_____

_____

_____

_____

D. Has despondency or depression been an element in your journey with God? What do you perceive was God's purpose? Is there a certain Scripture you use to resist the devil when you're hit with despondency?

_____

_____

_____

_____

E. If you've experienced perplexity, write down the issues that have perplexed you most. Is there anything from Abraham's story that comforts you in your perplexity?

_____

_____

_____

F. Have you ever gone through a relational crisis with others in the body of Christ? In what ways did God possibly design those conflicts? What was He after? How did the Lord help you to remain connected to the body? Is your heart free of all bitterness?

_____

_____

_____

_____

G. *Even when relationships get hard, remain in fellowship with believers so that God might be glorified through your life.* Write down, as a prayer to the Lord, how you're resolving to respond to that statement.

_____

_____

_____

23 SMALL GROUP DISCUSSION

(choose from these questions)

A. In the wilderness section of this chapter, glance over the elements of wilderness listed. Which one might you want to talk about with the group?

B. Share with the group how God has used loneliness redemptively in your life.

C. Let's talk about despondency and depression. Do you agree that there's part of it we need to resist and part of it we need to harness?

D. Has God ever blown your theological circuits with perplexity? Talk about it.

E. The fact that you're in this small group study confirms that you value the importance of staying connected to the body of Christ. How important is this small group to you?

F. Is there a certain seed (word of God) that has been working in your heart this past week?

G. Closing prayer.
   1. Are there any areas of sin or struggle in your life that you want to confess, according to James 5:16, so we can pray for you?
   2. Pray for anyone in the group who might be struggling with loneliness or despondency.

NOTES

Chapter 24
This Is the Big One

SELF-REFLECTION QUESTIONS

A. The author suggests there's one crisis in the life of a believer that's bigger than all others, and that opens to hundredfold fruitfulness when we navigate it successfully. Do you agree with this understanding of God's ways? Has there been a big crisis in your life?

_____
_____
_____
_____

B. Have you ever been in a trial that seemed disproportionately intense compared to the issues God seemed to be addressing in your life? As you endured through the perplexity, what did you learn?

_____
_____
_____
_____
_____

C. Look at these two verses, as well as the verses that surround them:
- "He weakened my strength in the way; He shortened my days" (Ps 102:23).
- "It is good for a man to bear the yoke in his youth" (Lam 3:27).

In what ways do you think these verses might be pointing to the sixtyfold crisis?

_____
_____
_____

D. For a more in-depth study of the two crisis points, go to Song of Solomon 3:1-5 and Song of Solomon 5:1-6:3. These two tests reflect the Bride's thirtyfold and sixtyfold tests respectively. What were the issues the Bridegroom was after in the Bride? How did these two great crises bring her into the hundredfold fruitfulness of Song of Solomon 8:11-12?

_____

_____

_____

_____

_____

E. The author said that some believers don't progress beyond thirtyfold fruitfulness because there's something they won't nail to the cross. Have you ever known someone who seemed to stay around thirtyfold fruitfulness for decades? Did you learn anything from their example?

_____

_____

_____

_____

F. The author suggested that in order to enter the sixtyfold crisis you have to *ask for more*. If you ever prayed a dangerous prayer, such as *Whatever it takes*, write about it here. In what way did that prayer take you on a journey with God you hadn't anticipated?

_____

_____

_____

_____

_____

G. How do you feel about dangerous prayers? Do you recommend them? Or do you think it's better not to ask?

_____

_____

_____

SMALL GROUP DISCUSSION
(choose from these questions)

A. Talk about the author's suggestion that there are typically two great trials in a believer's life. Does anyone have a story to support or contradict that?

B. Psalm 119:83 says, "For I have become like a wineskin in smoke." If a wineskin is exposed to smoke, it will probably not be useful for holding wine because the smoky fragrance will compromise the flavor of the wine. What do you think the psalmist meant by *a wineskin in smoke*?

C. *Some saints seem to camp at a certain level of fruitfulness and just hang there for years.* Talk about that statement, and your desire to keep moving forward in God.

D. From what you know of Job's story, what do you think he may have asked for? (see Job 12:4)

E. Do you think it's dangerous to say to the Lord, "Whatever it takes"? Should we pray dangerous prayers?

F. Was there a statement in this chapter that you'd like to highlight to the group?

G. Closing prayer.
   1. Are there any areas of sin or struggle in your life that you want to confess, according to James 5:16, so we can pray for you?
   2. Does anyone have a bold or dangerous prayer they want to offer to God?

NOTES

Chapter 25
Two Personal Stories

SELF-REFLECTION QUESTIONS

A. The author said that, when he was twenty-two, God was after his *self-determination* (the pride of making his own way in life). Is self-determination a part of the self-life that God targets sometimes in young people? Is there something about *your* self-life that God has brought to the cross? (e.g. self-centeredness, self-love, self-gratification, self-preservation, self-esteem, self-pity, self-image, self-seeking, etc.)

_____
_____
_____
_____

B. The author connects his sixtyfold crisis to a physical affliction he has endured. In your understanding of God's ways, does God sometimes use physical affliction as a catalyst to move us forward in our maturity? Do you view Hebrews 12:1-13 as supporting this? If so, in what way?

_____
_____
_____
_____

C. Peter wrote, "Beloved, do not think it strange concerning the fiery trial which is to try you, as though some strange thing happened to you" (1 Peter 4:12). Have you ever experienced a trial that seemed very strange to you? What was it? How did this verse help you?

_____
_____
_____
_____

D. *He's not simply teaching you something, He's training you.* Do you see a difference between teaching and training? How would you describe the difference? In your answer, you may want to reflect on Hebrews 12:11, "Now no chastening seems to be joyful for the present, but painful; nevertheless, afterward it yields the peaceable fruit of righteousness to those who have been trained by it."

_____

_____

_____

_____

E. *There are some keys you must have scars to handle.* Write your comments about that statement. In your comments, you may want to reflect on Revelation 1:18, "I am He who lives, and was dead, and behold, I am alive forevermore. Amen. And I have the keys of Hades and of Death."

_____

_____

_____

_____

F. How would you express to the Lord—today—the reach of your heart for hundredfold fruitfulness? Write your prayer here.

_____

_____

_____

G. The purpose of this book is not to show you how to gain victory over every patch of hardness in your heart, or over every stone of compromise, or over every weed that chokes your fruitfulness. Rather, the purpose of this book is to help you *recognize* them. Once you identify those hindrances, then you can get out your hoe, shovel, and sickle, and go after them as the Lord enables and leads you. Stay connected to other disciples, like the ones you've enjoyed in this group, who will help you to keep walking forward in victory. Write down how you intend to stay connected to other disciples in the body of Christ, even after this study in the parable of the sower is completed. Can you name the person or people you're going to continue to walk with?

_____

_____

_____

_____

SMALL GROUP DISCUSSION

(choose from these questions)

A. The author described hundredfold fruitfulness as *a place of greater love, greater intimacy, greater understanding, greater authority, and greater power.* In what way might that describe the reach of your soul?

B. If this study in the parable of the sower has been a blessing to you, one way that can be multiplied is for you to lead a small group through this study yourself. Do you feel led of the Lord to consider leading a small group through this study?

C. Would you like to talk about one of the questions in the Self-Reflection section above?

D. Was there a statement in this chapter that you'd like to highlight to the group?

E. Is there a certain seed (word of God) that has been working in your heart this past week?

F. Closing prayer.
   1. Are there any areas of sin or struggle in your life that you want to confess, according to James 5:16, so we can pray for you?
   2. In what way can we support you today in prayer?

NOTES

Chapter 26
Summary: Best Practices for Disciples

SELF-REFLECTION QUESTIONS

A. Review the bulleted *best practices for disciples* from Part One. Choose three or four from that list, write them down here, and why they are meaningful to you.

_____
_____
_____
_____
_____
_____

B. Review the best practices from Part Two. Choose three or four from that list, write them down here, and why they are meaningful to you.

_____
_____
_____
_____
_____
_____

C. Review the best practices from Part Three. Choose three from that list, write them down here, and why they are meaningful to you.

_____
_____
_____
_____

D. Review the best practices from Part Four. Choose three from that list, write them down here, and why they are meaningful to you.

___

___

___

___

___

___

E. Review the best practices from Part Five. Choose three or four from that list, write them down here, and why they are meaningful to you.

___

___

___

___

___

___

F. From the time you started this study in the parable of the sower, in which areas of discipleship have you seen the most fruitful progress in your life personally?

___

___

___

___

26 SMALL GROUP DISCUSSION

(choose from these questions)

A. Look over the practices of disciples in the listing of Part One, and tell the group which one is most meaningful to you right now.

B. Look over the practices of disciples in the listing of Part Two, and tell the group which one is most meaningful to you right now.

C. Look over the practices of disciples in the listing of Part Three, and tell the group which one is most meaningful to you right now.

D. Look over the practices of disciples in the listing of Part Four, and tell the group which one is most meaningful to you right now.

E. Look over the practices of disciples in the listing of Part Five, and tell the group which one is most meaningful to you right now.

F. Does anyone have an idea for how we can keep these best practices for disciples on our radar as we grow in fruitfulness through the years?

G. Closing prayer.

1. Are there any areas of sin or struggle in your life that you want to confess, according to James 5:16, so we can pray for you?
2. In what specific way do you currently desire to be more fruitful? We'll pray for you.

NOTES

Appendix
Fruitfulness Versus Talents
SELF-REFLECTION QUESTIONS

A. According to the author, *God loves us too much to give us talents we can't properly steward.* We might be inclined to measure God's love for us based upon the talents He gives us, but perhaps we should also see the measure of His love in the talents He *doesn't* give us. Have you ever felt God's love for you in the way He withheld a certain talent from you? What would have happened to you if He had given you a talent that was heavier than your frame could sustain?

_____

_____

_____

_____

B. *Talents refer to abilities and capacities; fruitfulness refers to how effectively we use our capacities for eternal value.* Admittedly, the author stammered in this chapter to distinguish between talents and fruit. Do you have a better way to distinguish them?

_____

_____

_____

C. The author maintains that a one-talent Christian functioning at hundredfold fruitfulness is likely to be more effective in the kingdom than a five-talent Christian functioning at thirtyfold fruitfulness. Write down whether you agree, and why. Can you think of situations with actual people that illustrate this idea?

_____

_____

_____

_____

D. Besides Joseph and Jesus, can you think of someone in the Bible who had five talents and was also hundredfold fruitful? Write down their name, the passage of Scripture that contains their story, and any observations you might have about their fruitfulness.

_____

_____

_____

_____

_____

E. As you've worked your way through this chapter, do you perceive yourself as a one- or two- or five-talent person? Is this evaluation helpful? Why or why not?

_____

_____

_____

F. *A one-talent woman who thought her motherhood was forever stripped from her became, through her devotion to God, a spiritual mother to millions.* How does this perspective on Anna inspire you? Have you sometimes thought of yourself as a one-talent person? If so, will you never again despise your one talent? Will you refuse to bury it (Matt 25:18)? How does Anna's story or Joseph's story give you hope for your own fruitfulness?

_____

_____

_____

_____

_____

_____

A SMALL GROUP DISCUSSION

(choose from these questions)

A. Let's talk about the talents God has given us. How would you identify and name some of the talents God has given you? Do you see a talent in someone else in the group that they didn't mention?

B. Now let's talk about the talents God *hasn't* given us. Are you grateful to God for a talent He *didn't* give you?

C. *Five talents are not available to all, but hundredfold fruitfulness is.* In what way does that statement help or encourage you?

D. Can you think of someone in the Bible who was talented but not fruitful? Or perhaps someone who was not very talented at all, but exceedingly fruitful?

E. *Fruitfulness is to be desired more than talents.* Let's talk about that idea. Does it make the parable of the sower glisten with even greater brilliance?

F. What can we glean from this chapter that will help us stop comparing our talents with those of others?

G. Closing prayer.
   1. Are there any areas of sin or struggle in your life that you want to confess, according to James 5:16, so we can pray for you?
   2. Express to the Lord your gratefulness for how this study in the parable of the sower has blessed and strengthened you.
   3. Does anyone in our group intend to lead another group of disciples through this curriculum on the parable of the sower? If so, let's bless them in prayer as they prepare to make disciples Jesus' way.

H. Leaders, please go to FruitfulHeart.net and submit a testimonial about what God did in your group. We'll post your testimonial to that page. You'll help other leaders understand how this study could benefit their small group.

NOTES

Fruitful Heart Curriculum

The Fruitful Heart Curriculum consists of two books:

- *SECRETS OF A FRUITFUL HEART*: Tools for Spiritual Growth from Jesus' Parable of the Sower
- Secrets of a Fruitful Heart: *DISCIPLESHIP MANUAL*

SECRETS OF A FRUITFUL HEART is a powerful exploration of Jesus' Parable of the Sower. When used with the *DISCIPLESHIP MANUAL*, these two books are a profound discipleship curriculum.

The wayside soil represents places in our hearts that have been trampled hard. The stones represent pockets of compromise that hinder our roots. The weeds represent cares and pleasures that choke our fruitfulness. With three powerful images, Jesus gave us His model of discipleship. When we soften our hearts, remove our stones, and cut back our weeds, our hearts become increasingly fruitful to God.

The *DISCIPLESHIP MANUAL* is written to help small discipleship groups go deeper in the parable. With each chapter, disciples answer questions that make the parable relevant for our lives. Then, when the group comes together, the Manual provides Discussion Questions that are relevant to every disciple. You'll be surprised at what you learn and discover just by interacting in your group with the questions.

For more information or quantity orders, go to www.FruitfulHeart.net. Make disciples Jesus' way!

Books by Bob Sorge

Discipleship
Secrets of a Fruitful Heart
Secrets of a Fruitful Heart: Discipleship Manual
Secrets of the Secret Place
Secrets of the Secret Place: Companion Study Guide
A Covenant With My Eyes
Stuck: Help for the Troubled Home

Prayer
Secrets of the Secret Place (paperback & hardcover)
Secrets of the Secret Place: Companion Study Guide
Secrets of the Secret Place: Leader's Manual
Reset: 20 Ways to a Consistent Prayer Life
Unrelenting Prayer
Illegal Prayers
Power of the Blood
Minute Meditations

Worship
Exploring Worship: A Practical Guide to Praise and Worship
Exploring Worship Workbook & Discussion Guide
Glory: When Heaven Invades Earth
Following The River: A Vision for Corporate Worship
Next Wave: Worship in a New Era

Enduring Faith
In His Face
The Fire Of Delayed Answers
The Fire Of God's Love
Pain, Perplexity, & Promotion: A Prophetic Interpretation of the Book of Job
Opened From the Inside: Taking the Stronghold of Zion

God's Still Writing Your Story
The Chastening of the Lord: The Forgotten Doctrine
The Cross: Never Too Dead for Resurrection
It's Not a Tomb It's a Womb
Sometimes We Need Trials

Leadership
Dealing With the Rejection and Praise of Man
Envy: The Enemy Within
Loyalty: The Reach Of The Noble Heart
It's Not Business It's Personal

For info on each title, go to oasishouse.com
Call Oasis House at 816-767-8880

Bob's books are also available at:
    christianbook.com
    amazon.com
    Kindle, iBooks, Nook, Google Play
    Audible

Stay connected with Bob at:
    fruitfulheart.net
    oasishouse.com
    YouTube.com/bobsorge
    Facebook.com/BobSorgeMinistry
    Blog: bobsorge.com
    Instagram: bob.sorge
    Twitter.com/BOBSORGE

Secrets of the Secret Place Curriculum

In addition to the Fruitful Heart Curriculum, Bob Sorge has written another discipleship curriculum that is being used around the world: *SECRETS OF THE SECRET PLACE*.

Bob's Secret Place Curriculum consists of four materials:

1. Secrets of the Secret Place
This book on our quiet time with Jesus is one of the leading resources worldwide for helping believers establish a secret place relationship with Jesus. Available in both paperback and hardcover.

2. Companion Study Guide
The *Secrets of the Secret Place Companion Study Guide* is useful for both private and group study. Discussion questions help a group engage with the content of each chapter.

3. Secrets Video Course

The secret place video course, taught by Bob Sorge, consists of twelve 30-minute sessions. This video series adds interest to a group study and strengthens the message of the book. The series can be purchased in DVD format, or streamed for free on YouTube—see Bob Sorge's YouTube Channel.

4. Leader's Manual

Almost anyone can lead a group through the Secrets Video Series simply by using the *Leader's Manual*. You'll receive guidelines for leading the group, along with handouts for each person. Photocopy and distribute the handouts for each person to complete while watching the film. The *Leader's Manual* is available in booklet form, or may be downloaded on the *Free Downloads* page at www.oasishouse.com.

This Secret Place Curriculum is an unparalleled tool for equipping believers in the necessity and magnificence of a secret place relationship with Jesus. Get your small group onto this! www.oasishouse.com

Secrets of a Fruitful Heart: DISCIPLESHIP MANUAL
Copyright 2024 by Bob Sorge
Published by Oasis House
PO Box 522
Grandview, MO 64030-0522
816-767-8880

Unless otherwise indicated, all Scripture quotations are from the New King James Version of the Bible. Copyright © 1979, 1980, 1982, Thomas Nelson Inc., Publisher. Used by permission.

All rights reserved. This book or parts thereof may not be reproduced in any form, except for brief quotations in reviews, without written permission from the publisher.

ISBN: 978-1-937725-70-9

Editor: Edie Mourey
Cover design: Jessica Beedle
Typesetter: Dale Jimmo

Stay connected with Bob at: fruitfulheart.net
oasishouse.com
YouTube.com/bobsorge
Facebook.com/BobSorgeMinistry
Blog: bobsorge.com
Instagram: bob.sorge
Twitter.com/BOBSORGE